This is a Parragon Publishing Book
This edition published in 2002

Parragon Publishing
Queen Street House
4 Queen Street
Bath BA1 1HE, UK

ISBN 0-75259-161-4

Printed in China.

Produced by
Monkey Puzzle Media Ltd

Sports
Heroes

Written by Jason Hook
Illustrated by Adam Hook

p

Contents

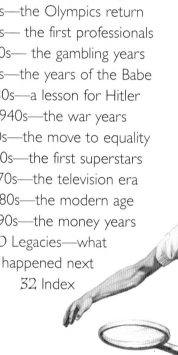

Who was the "father of football"?

WALTER CAMP, A PLAYER AND coach at Yale. In the 1880s, he introduced many of the rules that are still used in the modern game. These included a system for scoring points, a team of 11 instead of 15 (as in rugby), the quarterback position, the line of scrimmage, and the idea that a team had to give up the ball if they did not advance by enough yards after a number of downs.

Walter Camp followed a strict regime of physical training, and self denial and was an oustanding all-round athlete.

What are the Queensberry Rules?
They are 12 rules of modern boxing, written in 1867 by John Graham Chambers and named after the Marquis of Queensberry. They introduced three-minute rounds, one-minute rests, the ten-second count, and gloves.

What are "All-American" teams?
All-American teams are picked at the end of each season to indicate which college players have performed best in which position. The idea was pioneered by Walter Camp, who announced the first All-American football teams in 1889.

Who invented lacrosse?

Lacrosse was invented by Native Americans in Canada, who called it "baggataway." Games played by the Iroquois tribe could last three days. There were up to 1,000 players on each team, and one of the aims was to disable as many of your opponents as possible. A modern version became the national sport of Canada and was introduced to the U.S. in 1868.

Who umpired and made the rules for the first real game of baseball?

A New York City surveyor named Alexander J. Cartwright developed 20 rules. In 1846, he umpired the first game using nine-player teams and a diamond with four bases. Fielders could run a batter out by tagging him, instead of by throwing the ball at him, as in the British game of cricket.

How was the first basketball game played?

It was played using a soccer ball, with two peach buckets nailed to the walls of a YMCA gym. A ladder was used to retrieve the ball after a basket was scored. It was invented by Canadian James Naismith in 1891.

What did John Reid and six friends form in 1888?

They formed the United States' first golf club, St. Andrews, using a three-hole course in a New York cow pasture. The first member was Robert Lockhart, a linen merchant who had brought the clubs and balls back from Scotland.

When was the first great international boxing match?

It was fought with bare knuckles on April 17, 1860, between John C. Heenan of the U.S. and English champion Tom Sayers. The referee vanished when the crowd stormed the ring, and after 42 rounds it was called a draw.

Abner Doubleday is said to have devised the present-day playing positions of baseball.

Who was Abner Doubleday?

ACCORDING TO LEGEND, ARMY CADET DOUBLEDAY INVENTED BASEBALL in the summer of 1839, in a cow field in Cooperstown, New York. This is why the Baseball Hall of Fame was built there. In fact, the game played by Doubleday was more like the English game of rounders.

5

Who was the "Boston Strong Boy"?

THE GREAT JOHN L. SULLIVAN, WHO BECAME THE LAST World Heavyweight Boxing Champion of the bare-knuckle era by knocking out Paddy Ryan in nine rounds in 1882. He once won a 75-round fight in temperatures of up to 104°F (40°C). He was the first sporting hero to be paid to advertise products, and earned over $1 million during his career. Sport magazine called him: "A hero among heroes."

Who was the first professional football player?
William "Pudge" Heffelfinger became the first professional football player when Allegheny Athletic Club paid him $500 to join them. Playing as a guard for Yale, he had been picked for the All-American teams for the previous three years.

Did Heffelfinger enjoy football?
It would appear so. Heffelfinger was the first blocker to protect the ballcarrier by providing "interference." He spoke of "the fierce elation that comes from throwing your body across an opponent's knees and feeling him hit the turf with a solid crack."

John L. Sullivan knocked Paddy Ryan out in the 9th round of the World Heavyweight Championship of 1882 in less than 11 minutes.

When did baseball's Major Leagues begin?
Baseball's National League was founded in 1876. In 1900, the Western League was renamed the American League by its president, Ban Johnson. These two leagues became the Major Leagues.

How did Walker Breeze Smith win one of the United States' first golf matches?
He told his opponent, John C. Ten Eyck, that the secret was to keep your eye on the ball. He then promptly removed his glass eye, balanced it on the ball, and teed off.

When was the first U.S. Open Golf Championship?
The first U.S. Open was played in 1895. When Fred Herd won the trophy in 1898, the United States Golf Association made him put down a deposit for the trophy. Golfers had such a bad reputation at that time, that they thought he might pawn it!

What did Harry Decker invent?
Decker was the inventor of the padded catcher's glove used in baseball. These gloves were known as "deckers" for many years.

How did the Civil War affect baseball?
During the Civil War, Union soldiers from New York City played the game wherever the fighting took them. In this way, they spread the rules used by the first real team—Alexander Cartwright's New York Knickerbocker Baseball Club.

Who was baseball's first legend?

CAP ANSON, WHO MADE HIS DEBUT IN THE NEW NATIONAL LEAGUE for the Chicago White Stockings (now white sox) in 1876. He was the first player to make 3,000 hits, and played professional baseball for 27 years. A candy bar and a cigarette were named after him, and a reporter wrote, "He stood at first base like a mighty oak ... the symbol of all that was strong and good in baseball."

Adrian C. "Cap" Anson played in first base from 1879.

Which hero of baseball made his debut in 1890?

CY YOUNG, WHO MANY CONSIDER TO BE THE greatest pitcher ever, made his debut for Cleveland. Born Denton True Young, in Ohio, he went on to win an all-time record 511 Major League games during his career.

Cy Young claimed never to have been sick until he caught the flu at the age of 79.

Why did James Connolly almost not win his Olympic medal?
He misunderstood the Greek calendar during the 1896 Olympics in Athens, Greece, and stayed up celebrating for the whole night before his historic track and field event.

What did James B. Connolly receive in 1896?
Connolly received the first Olympic winner's medal awarded since Barasdates of Greece won the boxing in AD 393. The Olympics were revived at Athens in 1896 by Frenchman Baron Pierre de Coubertin, after a gap of 1,503 years. A triple jumper from Harvard, Connolly received a silver medal for winning. Gold was considered vulgar, and was not used for winner's medals until 1904.

Gentleman Jim beat John L. Sullivan in 1892 for a purse of $25,000.

Which great jockey invented the crouching position used by jockeys today?

Tod Sloan, from Indiana, invented the "monkey crouch." It was more comfortable for him to ride with short stirrups and his head almost on the horse's neck, because he had incredibly short legs.

Why was baseball's pitching mound moved from 50 ft (15 m) to 60 ft, 6 in (18.5 m) from the batter?

Because pitcher Rusie Amos, the "Hoosier Thunderbolt," pitched so fast that it was unfair on the batters. His catcher had to wear a sheet of lead in his glove.

How did Jim Corbett change boxing?

He was known as the "father of scientific boxing" for his skill inside the ring. He was also nicknamed the "California Dandy" for his elegant appearance outside the ring. Both of these qualities helped to make boxing popular with the public.

What did Dr. Coburn Haskell invent in 1898?

Haskell, a dentist from Cleveland, was playing with a bundle of rubber bands when his idea struck him. He invented a golf ball, filled with twisted rubber bands, so it flew much further than previous balls.

How did professional basketball develop?

The National Basketball League (NBL) was formed in 1898. It started as an attempt to find opponents who could take on the brilliant Trenton team of the YMCA League.

What did "Gentleman Jim" win in 1892?

"GENTLEMAN JIM" CORBETT KNOCKED OUT JOHN L. SULLIVAN IN NEW Orleans to win the first World Heavyweight Championship fought with gloves under Queensberry rules. Sullivan was unfit, but was not knocked out until the 21st round.

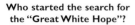

How did President Roosevelt change the shape of football?

IN 1905, PRESIDENT ROOSEVELT insisted that a bone-breaking, battering-ram formation called the "flying wedge" should be banned from the game. He did it after 18 players were killed in the previous season!

President Roosevelt was a great football fan.

What did May Sutton wear to cause trouble at Wimbledon?
In 1905, because she was only 18, May Sutton was allowed to wear a dress that did not cover up her ankles. This glimpse of the Californian youngster's legs caused a lot of trouble at the All-England Club. Her tennis also upset the British, as she went on to become the first non-English player to win Wimbledon.

Why did Jack Johnson flee from the U.S. in 1912?
He had been convicted of breaking a law by crossing state lines with his wife before they were married. Johnson fled, disguised as a member of a black baseball team, and defended his title abroad.

Who won the first World Series?

The first World Series was played in 1903, between the winners of the National League and the new American League. Cy Young pitched the Boston Red Sox to a 5—3 victory over Pittsburgh.

Honus Wagner once said, "There isn't much to being a ballplayer, if you're a ballplayer."

Why was Cy Young perfect in 1904?

He pitched the first ever perfect game in baseball history, playing for the Boston Red Sox against the Philadelphia Athletics. Not a single Philadelphia batter reached first base on either a hit or a walk.

How did Charles Follis become the first black professional football player?

Follis agreed to join the Shelby team in exchange for being given a job in a hardware store in 1904. He became known as the "Black Cyclone," and was a major star of the Ohio League.

Which Olympic champion was punched for jumping on a Sunday?

Alvin Kranzlein won his fourth gold medal with a record-breaking long jump at the 1904 Paris Olympics in France. Previous record-holder Meyer Prinstein, who had refused to compete because the event was on a Sunday, ran up and socked him!

Who won a famous marathon by coming second?

Johnny Hayes, a sales clerk at Bloomingdales, finished 0.75 seconds behind Italian Dorando Pietri in the marathon at the London Olympics of 1908 in England. But Pietri was disqualified, because British officials had carried him over the line after he collapsed!

Who appears on the most valuable baseball card?

HONUS WAGNER, THE GREAT PITTSBURGH SHORTSTOP WHO LED THE LEAGUE in batting for eight seasons from 1900 to 1911. The 1909 card bearing his image was withdrawn because Wagner, who was against smoking, thought it set a bad example for children to see the cards in packs of cigarettes.

Why did Ty Cobb keep a gun beside his bed?
Cobb's heroes were the aggressive rulers Napoleon and Caesar, and he ruled in a similar way on the baseball park. He upset so many players that he needed the gun to protect himself from his own teammates!

Which Native American won two Olympic golds?

J IM THORPE, WHOSE NATIVE AMERICAN NAME WAS WA-THO-HUCK, meaning "Bright Path." He followed a very bright path at the 1912 Stockholm Olympics, setting records in the Decathlon and Pentathlon. King Gustav of Sweden told him: "You are the greatest athlete in the world," to which Thorpe replied: "Thanks, King!" Thorpe's medals were tragically taken back because he had been paid $2 a game to play baseball—and was therefore not an amateur.

Jim Thorpe was voted outstanding male athlete of the first 50 years of the last century.

Who was the "Georgia Peach"?
This was the nickname of Ty Cobb, one of the most feared and ferocious players ever. Cobb played 22 seasons with the Detroit Tigers of the American League. He led the league in batting for nine consecutive years from 1907 to 1915, and has the all-time best batting average (.367). His aggressive style was shown in his career total of 892 stolen bases, a record which lasted until 1979.

What did Marshall Foch say about football?

Marshall Foch, the Frenchman who commanded the Allied Forces during World War I, said of a football game between the Army and Navy—"Mon Dieu, this game is war! It has everything."

What was the "Battle of the Camera Shot"?

The fight in which Jack Johnson was defeated by Jess Willard in 1915. Johnson claimed that a camera shot of him shading his eyes from the Sun after his knockout proved that he had lost the fight deliberately and had not really been knocked out.

What scandal shocked baseball fans in 1919?

The "Black Sox" scandal. After the Chicago White Sox lost the 1919 World Series to the Cincinatti Reds, eight players were accused of throwing the game for gamblers' money. They were acquitted, but were banned for life anyway.

Which shop assistant started a popular golfing boom?

Francis Ouimet, who in 1913 became the first amateur to win the U.S. Open. He beat famous British professionals Harry Vardon and Ted Ray in a play-off. His caddy was only 10 years old!

Who became a football legend in only four years?

George Gipp, fullback for the famous Notre Dame college team. He became a national celebrity in a four-year career (1917—1920). He died, at the age of 25, after playing a game while sick with a temperature of 102°F (39°C).

"Shoeless" Joe Jackson was one of the best hitters ever in baseball.

Who was "Shoeless" Joe Jackson?

A GREAT HITTER, WHO ONCE PLAYED IN SOCKS BECAUSE HIS NEW SHOES GAVE him blisters. He was the most popular player banned in the Black Sox scandal, causing the public to cry— "Say it ain't so, Joe!"

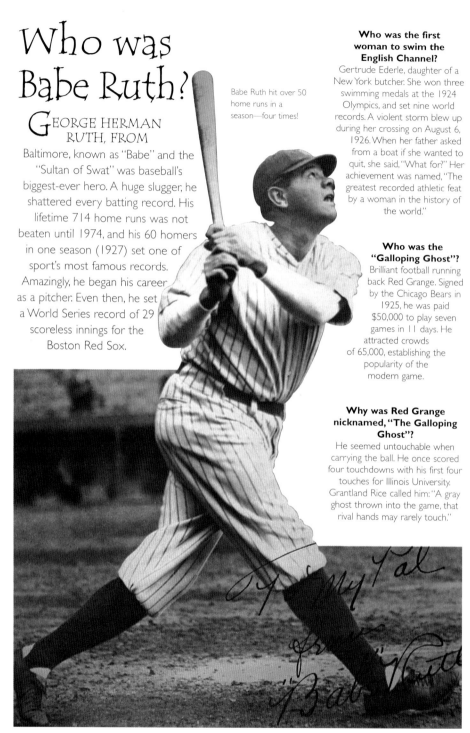

Who was Babe Ruth?

GEORGE HERMAN RUTH, FROM

Baltimore, known as "Babe" and the "Sultan of Swat" was baseball's biggest-ever hero. A huge slugger, he shattered every batting record. His lifetime 714 home runs was not beaten until 1974, and his 60 homers in one season (1927) set one of sport's most famous records. Amazingly, he began his career as a pitcher. Even then, he set a World Series record of 29 scoreless innings for the Boston Red Sox.

Babe Ruth hit over 50 home runs in a season—four times!

Who was the first woman to swim the English Channel?

Gertrude Ederle, daughter of a New York butcher. She won three swimming medals at the 1924 Olympics, and set nine world records. A violent storm blew up during her crossing on August 6, 1926. When her father asked from a boat if she wanted to quit, she said, "What for?" Her achievement was named, "The greatest recorded athletic feat by a woman in the history of the world."

Who was the "Galloping Ghost"?

Brilliant football running back Red Grange. Signed by the Chicago Bears in 1925, he was paid $50,000 to play seven games in 11 days. He attracted crowds of 65,000, establishing the popularity of the modern game.

Why was Red Grange nicknamed, "The Galloping Ghost"?

He seemed untouchable when carrying the ball. He once scored four touchdowns with his first four touches for Illinois University. Grantland Rice called him: "A gray ghost thrown into the game, that rival hands may rarely touch."

Helen Wills won gold medals in both singles and doubles tennis at the 1924 Olympic Games.

Who was "Little Miss Poker Face"?

Hⁿ ELEN WILLS, WHO WAS NAMED FOR HER
serious approach to tennis. It seemed to work. She did not drop a set between 1927 and 1932, and in her career she won seven U.S. titles and eight Wimbledons.

What was Walter Hagen's catchphrase?
"Don't hurry, don't worry, you're here only a short time, so be sure to smell the flowers." Hagen, who often played in the previous night's dinner suit, became golf's first millionaire by winning ten majors.

Why was Tarzan such a good swimmer?
In 19 movies of the 1930s, the role of Tarzan was played by Johnny Weissmüller. He had won three swimming golds at the 1924 Paris Olympics, and two more in 1928, and broke 67 world amateur records.

Why did the Harlem Globetrotters "globetrot"?
They had no court, so they traveled the U.S. in promoter Abe Saperstein's car. They started as a competitive side in 1927, but became a world-touring exhibition side. No black players were allowed in the NBA until 1950.

What law did heavyweight champ Jack Dempsey necessitate?
The rule saying a boxer has to retire to a neutral corner after a knockdown was introduced after Dempsey, the "Manassa Mauler", repeatedly knocked down Luis Firpo in a brutal 1923 fight.

What did Mildred "Babe" Didrikson achieve?

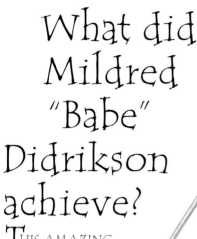

THIS AMAZING TEXAN won the gold and set world records in the javelin and 80 meters hurdles at the 1932 Los Angeles Olympics. She

Mildred Didrikson was nicknamed "Babe" after hitting 13 home runs against a boys team.

received the silver in the high jump because her "western roll" style was judged illegal! She played on three championship basketball teams, toured playing billiards, and once pitched out Joe DiMaggio. Didrikson later helped establish the women's golf tour, winning the Women's U.S. title three times.

Why did President Roosevelt squeeze Joe Louis' biceps?

In 1938, Louis was fighting German champion Max Schmeling. With war looming, Roosevelt told him, "We need muscles like yours to beat Germany." Louis won in one round.

Who was the first sportsman to have a bigger salary than the President?

Babe Ruth, who received $80,000 for the 1930 season. When asked why he deserved to earn more money than the President, Ruth said, "I had a better year!"

Who held the World Heavyweight Boxing title for the longest time?

The brilliant "Brown Bomber" Joe Louis. He won the title from James Braddock in 1937, and held it for 11 years, 8 months. He defended 25 times, against a series of "Bum of the Month" challengers.

Owen's long jump record was unbroken for 25 years, 79 days.

How long did it take Jesse Owens to set four world records?
About 45 minutes. Between 3:15 and 4:00 p.m. on May 25 1935, representing Ohio University, Owens set records in the 100 yards, 220 yards, 220 yard hurdles, and running broad jump.

What baseball record did Lou Gehrig set?
Between June 1, 1925 and May 2, 1939, the "Iron Horse" played 2,130 consecutive games for the New York Yankees. He ignored broken fingers and pulled muscles to set a record that lasted until 1995.

What was the first object placed in baseball's Hall of Fame?
When the Hall of Fame opened in 1936, the spikes of Ty Cobb, the first elected member, were put on display. Cobb sharpened his spikes so that he could leave fielders a reminder of his presence.

Which golfer won the "Impossible Quadrilateral"?
In 1930, Bobby Jones became the only golfer ever to win the old Grand Slam—or "Impossible Quadrilateral" as it was called—of U.S. Amateur, U.S. Open, British Amateur, and British Open titles of one year.

Was Bronco Nagurski the toughest football player ever?
Possibly. The Chicago Bears fullback (1930—1937) once bulldozed through opponents for a 45-yard touchdown, collided with the goalposts, and ran on into a brick wall. Regaining consciousness, he said, "That last guy hit me awfully hard."

How was Hitler taught a lesson at the 1936 Berlin Olympics?

HITLER HAD HOPED WHITE ATHLETES WOULD DEMONSTRATE THEIR racial supremacy. Black American athlete Jesse Owens, the 22-year-old son of cotton picker, had other ideas. He broke three Olympic records and equaled another in winning gold in the 100 meters, 200 meters, long jump and 4 × 100 meters relay. Hitler refused to present the medals. Owens remarked, "We lost no sleep over not being greeted by Adolf Hitler."

Joe DiMaggio (shown left of Mickey Mantle) was known for his graceful style.

How did the war affect sporting heroes?
Baseball stars enlisted, and the All-Star game was cancelled in 1945. Some football teams stopped playing. The Pittsburgh Steelers and Philadelphia Eagles merged as the "Steagles" for one season. Hockey overtime was banned. More women and black players became stars.

What was the lace panties scandal?
In 1949, "Gorgeous Gussy" Moran from California shocked Wimbledon by wearing a lace trim beneath a shorter than usual skirt. Designer Ted Tinling had to resign from his post as a Wimbledon official, but became famous as a dress designer.

Which golfing legend failed to win the U.S. Open?
Sam Snead won the 1946 British Open, three PGAs, and three Masters but could never win the US Open. He was runner-up four times, and in 1947 missed a 30-inch putt on the last hole.

Who was football's "Papa Bear"?
George Halas, who coached the Chicago Bears to a record 320 wins. In 1940, they scored a record NFL Championship victory of 73—0 against the Washington Redskins. At 66—0 they were asked not to convert a touchdown, because they had run out of balls!

What did Simon and Garfunkel sing about Joe DiMaggio?
In the 1968 song *Mrs Robinson*, they sang, "Where have you gone, Joe DiMaggio? / A nation turns its lonely eyes to you / What's that you say, Mrs. Robinson? / "Joltin" Joe has left and gone away."

Which baseball legend married Marilyn Monroe?

"JOLTIN" JOE DiMAGGIO, THE "YANKEE CLIPPER," A LEGENDARY SLUGGER
and fielder. In 1941, he hit safely in a record 56 straight games—a run that almost ended when his brother nearly caught him! This winning streak led to one of the nine World Series DiMaggio won with the New York Yankees. He married fellow legend Marilyn Monroe in 1954, but they divorced a short time later.

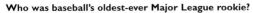

Who was baseball's oldest-ever Major League rookie?

Satchell Paige, who was signed from the Negro Leagues by the Cleveland Indians in 1948, age 42. A crowd of 72,000 watched his debut, and he went on to pitch in the Major League at the age of 59.

How did Sugar Ray Robinson get his name?

WALKER SMITH JR. BORROWED AN IDENTITY CARD FROM HIS friend, Ray Robinson, so he could fight when under-age. He was called "sweet as sugar." As "Sugar Ray Robinson" he was possibly the greatest boxer of all time.

What was the color barrier in baseball?

Black players were only allowed to play in the Negro Leagues, never in the Major Leagues. The unfairness of this situation became even clearer when black soldiers fought for the United States in World War II. The sporting hero who broke this barrier was Jackie Robinson, when he signed for the Brooklyn Dodgers in 1947. He won the first Rookie of the Year award, despite some white players refusing to play against him.

From 1943—51 Sugar Ray Robinson won 91 consecutive fights.

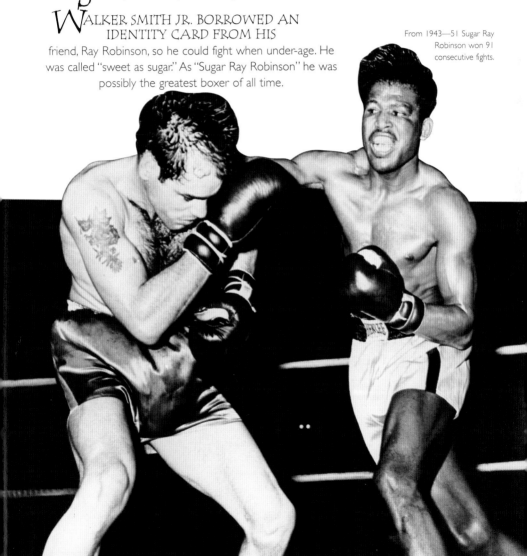

Who was the first black woman to win Wimbledon?

ALTHEA GIBSON, WHO WON THE TITLE IN 1957. GIBSON'S TALENT HAD BEEN spotted as a 13-year-old by the Police Athletic Supervisor, who bought her two secondhand rackets. She impressed U.S. tournaments, where campaigns had to be staged to allow black players to compete. In her career, Gibson won two Wimbledons, two U.S. Championships, and one French title.

Who collapsed in the 10th round of a 1952 Sugar Ray Robinson fight?
The referee! This fight against Joey Maxim at Yankee Stadium for the light-heavyweight championship was the only one in which Robinson was ever stopped. He retired with heat exhaustion in the 13th round.

Why did Ben Hogan offer to get his lawnmower?
Golf's "Ice Man" won one British Open, four U.S. Opens, two PGAs, and two Masters. When he won the British Open at Carnoustie, Scotland, he said of the long grass on the greens, "I've got a lawnmower back in Texas. I'll send it over."

Who was the only unbeaten heavyweight champion?
The "Brockton Blockbuster" Rocky Marciano. He won the title from Jersey Joe Walcott in 1952, and ended his career with 49 wins, 42 knockouts, and 0 losses— despite a short reach that meant he sometimes had to jump to land punches.

How did "Little Mo" get her name?
Big-hitting Maureen Connolly, who won tennis's Grand Slam in 1953, was named after "Big Mo"—the U.S. battleship *Missouri*. She won three U.S. titles and three Wimbledons before injury forced her into retirement at the age of only 19.

Althea Gibson was 30 when she won her first Wimbledon title.

Bill Russell was voted the NBA's Most Valuable Player five times.

What hat-trick did basketball's Bill Russell score in 1956?

In a single year, legendary center Bill Russell led the University of San Francisco to the college championship by winning their last 56 games; led the U.S. to gold at the Melbourne Olympics in Australia, then joined the Boston Celtics mid-season and helped them to the NBA title. Black players had not played in the NBA until 1950. Russell went on to win 11 titles in 13 years with the Celtics, and in 1966 became the NBA's first black coach.

Who was baseball's "Say Hey Kid"?
The legendary Willie Mays of the Giants, who used to address people with "Say, hey!" He hit 660 home runs in his joyous career, and his 460-ft- (140-meter-), over-the-shoulder catch in the 1954 World Series is one of baseball's magic moments.

Who hit the longest home run?
New York Yankees hero Mickey Mantle, who launched a 634-ft (193-meter) homer out of Briggs Stadium, Detroit, against the Detroit Tigers in September 1960. Mantle could hit homers either left-handed or right-handed, and led the league six times in runs.

Which baseball star was the cartoon character Yogi Bear named after?
The New York Yankees catcher Yogi Berra. He won 14 pennants in his 19-year career, and was also famous for making many memorable remarks, including, "It ain't over until it's over."

How successful was Otto Graham?
Graham was the most successful quarterback ever. In his 10-year career from 1946 to 1955, his team, the Cleveland Browns, won a conference title in every season and a league title in seven seasons.

How did Muhammad Ali lose his world heavyweight title?

In 1967, he was stripped of his title for refusing to join US conscription to fight in Vietnam. He said: "I don't have no quarrel with them Vietcongs."

Who lived in a penthouse with llama-fur carpets?

The flamboyant "Broadway" Joe Namath, the first quarterback to pass for 4,000 yards. In 1969, Namath promised that his New York Jets would beat hot favorites the Baltimore Colts in the Superbowl. They did, 16—7.

Did Roger Maris break Babe Ruth's record?

In 1961, Maris broke Ruth's hallowed record of 60 home runs in a season. However, he hit his 61st homer in the 162nd game, while Ruth's season lasted only 154 games. So, many people felt the Babe's record still stood.

When was the first Superbowl played?

In 1967, after the merger of the National Football League (formed in 1922) and the American Football League (formed 1960). The Green Bay Packers (NFL) beat the Kansas City Chiefs (AFL) 35—10 in the first annual Superbowl between the champions of each league.

Who was "The Greatest"?

Muhammad Ali claimed to be "the greatest," and went on to become the most famous sportsman on the planet. In 1964, when he was still known as Cassius Clay, he defeated heavyweight champion Sonny Liston, who was believed to be unbeatable. Clay converted to Islam, and adopted his new name. As Muhammad Ali, he lit up sport with his boxing skills, predictions of victory, playful boasting, and famous poems such as his claim that he could, "Float like a butterfly, sting like a bee."

After Bob Beamon's record-breaking long jump of over 29 ft (8.9 m), he never again jumped over 27 ft (8 m).

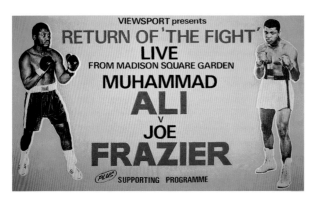

Muhammed Ali won 22 world title fights and lost three.

What did Bobby Jones say about Jack Nicklaus?

Jones famously said of "Golden Bear" Nicklaus: "He plays a game with which I am not familiar." Nicklaus, possibly the greatest golfer ever, won three British Open, four U.S., six Masters, and five PGA titles.

What was the "jump into the 21st Century"?

At THE 1968 MEXICO OLYMPICS, EVERYTHING CAME RIGHT FOR New York City's Bob Beamon. In the final of the long jump, he jumped beyond the gaze of the electronic measuring device. The judges used a tape measure to discover Beamon had leapt 29 feet (8.90 m), beating the world record by an astonishing 22 inches (55 cm). Beamon was so overcome, he collapsed. Another competitor said: "Compared to this jump, the rest of us are children."

What happened to Wilma Rudolph's shoes?
Wilma Rudolph won the gold in the 100 meters, 200 meters, and relay at the 1960 Rome Olympics. As a child, she had needed special shoes because of polio. Then her running shoes were stolen by souvenir hunters.

Who was Wilt the Stilt?
Wilt Chamberlain, the legendary basketball rival of Bill Russell. In 1962, the 7 ft 1 in (2.16 m) center became the first player to score 100 points in a game, for the Philadelphia Warriors. He later became a volleyball superstar.

Who is in the Hall of Fame for both football and lacrosse?
Jim Brown was one of the greatest college lacrosse players ever. He then led football rushing yardages in eight out of nine years for the Cleveland Browns from 1957 to 1965, setting a record for 12,312 yards rushing.

Mark Spitz
swimming butterfly.

What did Mark Spitz achieve at the 1972 Munich Olympics?

THE CALIFORNIAN SWIMMER WON SEVEN GOLD MEDALS AND set seven world records—two in freestyle, two in butterfly, and three in relays. As sport grew more commercial, Spitz retired and made money by appearing in advertisements for clothes, milk, hairdryers, and electric razors. He said of his seven golds, "The medals weighed a lot. They have heavy, crazy chains. Really, it was hard to stand up straight wearing them all."

Which athlete remained unbeaten for an amazing 10 years?
After victory in the World Cup 400 meters hurdles in 1977, Ed Moses won his next 122 races. During this time, he collected Olympic gold at Los Angeles in 1984 and broke the world record four times.

Who presented her opponent with a live pig?
Billie Jean King gave the pig to self-proclaimed male-chauvinist pig Bobby Riggs, before their famous 1973 "Battle of the Sexes" tennis match. An audience of 50 million television viewers watched King defeat ex-pro Riggs. Billie Jean King had helped women's tennis to gain proper recognition by winning an amazing 20 Wimbledon titles during her career: six singles, 10 doubles, four mixed doubles.

Who was known as "The Juice"?
O. J. Simpson, one of the most graceful runningbacks ever. Playing for the Buffalo Bills, he shattered Jim Brown's rushing record, and became the first player to rush for 2,000 yards in a season.

What great baseball record did "Hammering Hank" break?
In 1974, Henry Aaron hit his 715th career home run, overtaking the Babe's 714. The ball he hit it with is now in the Hall of Fame, and Aaron went on to set a career record of 755 homers.

What were the "Rumble in the Jungle" and the "Thrilla in Manilla"?
Two of Muhammad Ali's most famous fights. In the Rumble, in Zaire in 1974, Ali outwitted the enormous George Foreman to regain his title in eight rounds. In the Thrilla in 1975, he defeated Joe Frazier in 15 rounds.

How did Arthur Ashe prepare for his Wimbledon final?
By playing blackjack into the early hours. As a child, Arthur Ashe had been banned from tournaments in Virginia because of his color. In 1975, he beat Jimmy Connors to become the first black player to win the men's singles at Wimbledon.

Which engaged couple won five Grand-Slam tennis events?

I N 1974, 19-YEAR-OLD CHRIS EVERT WON THE FRENCH AND WIMBLEDON titles. Her fiancé, 20-year-old Jimmy Connors, won the Wimbledon, U.S., and Australian titles. They split up at the end of the year.

Why was dunking banned from college basketball in 1968?
To try to reduce the dominance of Lew Alcindor, who led UCLA to three college championships. After changing his name to Kareem Abdul-Jabbar, he broke all scoring records in helping the LA Lakers to five NBA championships.

Who is "Mr Hockey"?
Canadian Gordie Howe, who played 33 seasons of ice hockey, mainly for the Detroit Red Wings. He set the NHL record for points (1,809), won a WHA title playing alongside his two sons, and appeared in his 23rd All-Star game at the age of 51.

Connors was known for his powerful return of serve, Evert for her steady baseline play.

Who is the highest-rated quarterback ever?

JOE MONTANA, WHO WAS NAMED MVP IN THE NFL FOUR TIMES. HE MADE the San Francisco 49ers the team of the 80s, winning four Superbowls between 1982 and 1990. In the Championship game of 1982, he threw a famous play known as "The Catch". With a minute to play, losing 21—17, he threw a high pass to Dwight Clark for a touchdown. Montana said: "I don't know how he got it. He can't jump that high!"

One of the greatest-ever quarterbacks—Joe Montana.

Which ice hockey records does Wayne Gretsky hold?
Known simply as "The Great One," Gretsky dominated his sport more than any other team player in history. Playing for the Edmonton Oilers, and later the Los Angeles Kings, he was NHL scoring champion and MVP nine times. In 1980, aged 19, he became the youngest player to be the season's top scorer. When he retired in 1999, he held records for career goals, points, and assists.

Who lost only one tennis match in 1983?
Martina Navratilova, the Czech player who became a U.S. citizen in 1981. She set new standards for women's tennis, winning 18 major singles titles and a world-record 167 singles tournaments.

What was the Chicago Bears' "one-man gang"?
This was how *Sports Illustrated* described Walter Payton. Between 1975 and 1987, the Bears' legendary runningback rushed for a record 16,726 yards, and broke O. J. Simpson's single-game record.

Who said: "You are the pits of the world!"
Hot-tempered genius John McEnroe, who won three Wimbledons and four US Opens, but in 1990 became the first player to be disqualified from a Grand Slam tournament for verbally abusing an umpire.

What did Reggie Jackson say about the World Series?
"The only reason I don't like playing in the World Series is I can't watch myself play." Jackson was called "Mr October" because of his outstanding record in World Series—which are played in that month.

Why did Carl Lewis wear red stilettos?

For a tire advertisement. Lewis is possibly the athlete of

the century, with nine Olympic golds. He won four golds, broke the 100 meters record at the 1984 Games, and won the long jump in four consecutive Olympics.

How did Carl Lewis win Olympic gold by coming second?

In the 1988 Seoul Olympics in Korea, he was beaten in the 100 meters by Canadian Ben Johnson, who ran an astonishing 9.79 seconds. It was proved to be too astonishing—Johnson failed a drugs test and the gold went to Lewis.

Which sisters-in-law won four golds at the 1988 Olympics?

Florence "Flo-Jo" Griffith-Joyner, famous for her multi-colored fingernails, won the gold in the 100 meters, 200 meters, and relay sprints. Her sister-in-law Jackie Joyner-Kersee won the gold in the heptathlon with a world-record 7,291 points.

Why did basketball star of the 80s "Magic" Johnson retire in 1991?

He had been infected with the HIV virus. Combining height, speed, and skill, Johnson had transformed the position of guard, winning five championships with the LA Lakers, and setting a record for assists.

Carl Lewis stayed at the peak of condition for over ten years.

Which sporting hero defied gravity?
Basketball's greatest player, Michael Jordan, who became known as "His Airness" because he possessed an unbelievable ability to change direction in mid-air. He won six NBA Championships with the Chicago Bulls, and was MVP in every final. Jordan had the highest-ever scoring average, won two Olympic golds, earned the most money in sporting history ($300 million), and appeared on *Sports Illustrated*'s cover a record 42 times (beating Muhammad Ali's total of 34).

Which tennis star threw up on court?
"Pistol" Pete Sampras threw up on court during a fifth-set tiebreak against Alex Corretja, on his way to winning the U.S. Open in 1996. Sampras won Wimbledon six times in seven years, and has earned over $32 million in prize-money.

What happened to Nancy Kerrigan before the 1994 Winter Olympics?

THE ICE SKATER WAS ATTACKED AND struck on the knee to try to prevent her competing. Her arch-rival Tonya Harding was accused of being involved and was later sentenced to three years probation.

Nancy Kerrigan eventually won silver at the 1994 winter Olympics.

What happened in the 1997 Masters?

TIGER WOODS BECAME THE YOUNGEST GOLFER

to win the Masters, and the first black player to win a Major tournament. Woods had already won $1 million in only nine tournaments. He not only won the Masters, but hit a record 18 under par, and won by an astonishing 12 shots. The tournament is held in Augusta, whose founder Clifford Roberts once said, "As long as I'm alive, golfers will be white and caddies will be black."

What record did Mark McGwire shatter?

In 1998, McGwire broke the famous record for home runs in a season. He hit 70 homers for the St. Louis Cardinals to overtake both Babe Ruth and Roger Maris. The ball he hit for the last homer was sold for $2.7 million.

What did Greg Maddux and Pedro Martinez sign in 1997?

Maddux of the Atlanta Braves and Martinez of the Boston Red Sox each signed record contracts for $11.5 million a year. Maddux was the first player to win the Cy Young trophy for four consecutive years.

What did George Foreman win in 1994?

At the age of 45, the "punching preacher" became the oldest boxer to win a version of the world heavyweight title, by defeating Michael Moorer. He said, "I proved that 40 is no death sentence."

Who is Mia Hamm?

Probably the best female soccer player ever. She scored 103 goals between 1989 and 1994 as her university won four college championships and lost only one match. She played for the national team at the age of 15, and won the Women's World Cup at 19.

Who were the "dream team"?

Because of changes in the rules, professionals could compete in the 1992 Barcelona Olympics. The U.S. won the basketball gold by forming a "dream team" of sporting heroes including Michael Jordan and "Magic" Johnson.

Why was Mike Tyson fined a record $2,980,000?

He bit off part of Evander Holyfield's ear during their bout in 1997. Holyfield will be remembered as a dignified champion. Tyson, who became the youngest-ever heavyweight champ age 20 in 1986, will unfortunately be remembered for this incident and a three-year prison sentence for rape.

What happened to Jim Thorpe's Olympic medals in 1982?

The IOC finally admitted that it had been wrong, and returned Thorpe's gold medals to his family. Thorpe had died penniless in 1953. He was buried in Mauch Chunk, Pennsylvania, which changed its name to Jim Thorpe, and used his grave as a tourist attraction.

Why do no baseball players wear the number 42?

In 1997, Jackie Robinson's number was retired to celebrate the 50th anniversary of his breaking baseball's color barrier.

How did the great John L. Sullivan end his days?

Sullivan, who had been a very heavy drinker, ended up touring the country giving lectures on temperance.

Who lit the torch for the 1996 Atlanta Olympics?

Muhammad Ali, in a ceremony made more moving by his suffering from Parkinson's Syndrome. Ali became the first man to twice regain the heavyweight title when he defeated Leon Spinks in 1978. A later comeback against Larry Holmes in 1980, in which Ali retired after 10 rounds of punishment, contributed to this syndrome. In Atlanta, he moved slowly and his hands shook, but Ali retained extraordinary dignity.

What is the "House That Ruth Built"?

YANKEE STADIUM, BUILT IN 1923 WITH MONEY FROM THE AUDIENCES

Babe Ruth attracted. The Red Sox sold him to the New York Yankees for $125,000 in 1920. He led the Yankees four World Series, and christened the new stadium with a home run.

Which sporting heroes have trophies names after them?

You know that you have become a sporting legend when a trophy gets named after you. The Cy Young Award is given to each season's best pitcher. An award for best college football player is named after Walter Payton.

The Yankee Stadium is the home of baseball.

Why was Mildred Didrikson's last U.S. Open golf title so incredible?
She won by 12 strokes in 1954, only a year after having surgery for cancer. This remarkable sporting hero finally succumbed to the disease the following year.

Which sporting heroes went into showbusiness?
Many of them. Jack Johnson ended his days performing with a flea circus. Jesse Owens raced against horses to make a living. Jim Brown starred in the 1966 movie *The Dirty Dozen*.

O.J. Simpson was one of the sporting heroes of the seventies.

Which sporting hero faced a murder trial?

IN 1994, O. J. SIMPSON WAS ARRESTED, AFTER A TELEVISED POLICE CHASE, and charged with the brutal murder of his ex-wife Nicole Brown and her friend Ronald Goldman. Simpson had retired as a football player in 1979, and become a famous commentator and comic actor. His trial in 1995 was also televised and attracted huge publicity. In 1995, Simpson was controversially found not guilty.

Index

ACKNOWLEDGEMENTS

The photographs in this book were supplied
by: Allsport 1, 20, 24, 31; Camera Press 27 (F.
Callaghan), 28 (N. Lomax), 29 (F. Baron);
Corbis 6, 13, 25, 26; Peter Newark's Pictures
5, 9, 10, 14, 17, 18, 19, 22.